The Blue Door

James C. Hopkins & Yoko Danno

THE WORD WORKS
INTERNATIONAL EDITIONS
WASHINGTON, DC

First Edition   First Printing
The Blue Door
Copyright © 2006 by Yoko Danno & James C. Hopkins

Reproduction of any part of this book in any form or by any means, electronic or mechanical, including photocopying, must be with permission in writing from the publisher. Address inquiries to:

The WORD WORKS
PO Box 42164
Washington, DC 20015
editor@wordworksdc.com

Cover photograph by James C. Hopkins
Calligraphy on page 10 by Sonoye Iida

Book design, typography by Janice Olson

Library of Congress Number: 2005936773
International Standard Book Number: 0-915380-62-5

Acknowledgments

The following poems have appeared, sometimes in an earlier version, in the following journals:

Frantic Egg
    when the mist clears   (by James C. Hopkins)

Innisfree Poetry Journal
    the blue door   (by James C. Hopkins)
    night heron   (by James C. Hopkins)
    hopscotch   (by Yoko Danno)
    moon   (by Yoko Danno)
    departure   (by Yoko Danno)
    anima   (by Yoko Danno)
    crystal   (by Yoko Danno)

Kansai Time Out
    evening flower   (by Yoko Danno)

Mite: Poetry and Criticism
    click   (by Yoko Danno)

for Hilary Tham Goldberg

the Blue Door

When Yoko Danno was a young girl in Sasayama, Japan, a Buddhist monk at her family's ancestral shrine told her that she must learn to read and to write in English. Soon, she began studying with American missionaries. Eventually she went on to receive a degree in English Literature at a nearby college, and became part of a slightly eccentric, expatriate community of Western literati and early "Beat poets" in Japan. For the next forty years she wrote poems only in the English language.

Fifteen years ago, after finishing college, James C. Hopkins was living in Southern California. One afternoon, on the beach in front of his house, a small white dog ran up to him and began barking wildly. Soon the dog's owner appeared— a Japanese woman who, later that afternoon, offered him a job as a fashion model in Tokyo. He accepted and was soon learning basic Japanese from cassette audio-tapes while commuting on the LA freeways. In Japan, he abandoned hope of mastering the language, but discovered Buddhism and Japanese poetry.

Yoko Danno and James C. Hopkins met at a poetry retreat in a castle outside of Florence, Italy in the fall of 2001. James remembers only a glimpse of purple silk, and Yoko's journal entry simply recalls a "young man who seems to be very social"—but they instantly recognized familiar and complex worlds within each other, and met the next morning for a cup of green tea.

One night, while walking through the castle vineyards, they came across a tree on the crest of a hill, mysteriously bathed in rays of white light. The tree appeared to be burning at the bottom of a lake, but never seemed to be consumed. The next morning as they left for their own countries, Yoko gave James a white feather, and asked for one thing in return: a gift of five English words. He gave her "rooftop," "blue," "sparrow," "thankful," and "time."

Several days later, James received a poem from Japan which contained the five words that he had given. Attached to the message were five new words—Yoko's gift to him. The words were "fly," "swing," "sting," "clouds," and "turtle's eyes." A week later, Yoko received a poem from America. Over the course of the next nine months, from opposite sides of the planet, Yoko and James wrote more than fifty poems, woven together in this manner.

On the Summer Solstice of 2002, Yoko and James decided to change their method of collaboration. Each asked a simple question, and the other answered in the form of a poem. First, James asked Yoko, "What will you burn?" and, in return, Yoko asked James "What are your thoughts while watching lotus petals flowing down the river?" For the next year, they sent questions and answers around the world, until another fifty poems had been written.

In August 2003, James and Yoko met again, this time on the shore of lake Chuzenji-ko, in the mountainous Nikko region of Japan. They met during the week of the Obon Festival, when the spirits of the dead return to their old homes and are welcomed by the living with fresh flowers, food, and incense. For six days they wander their old rooms, and sleep in their old beds. On the seventh night they return to heaven, guided by huge mountaintop bonfires, set ablaze by the local monks.

For three days and nights Yoko and James sifted through the poems that they had written together over the past two years. One by one, they read each poem, and the writer of the poem had to say simply "yes" or "no." Then, one by one, the recipient of the poem had to decide "yes" or "no" as well. One by one, the sake bottles were removed by the hotel maids. At the end of this process, they were somehow left with exactly 22 poems written by Yoko, and 22 poems written by James. They took this as an auspicious sign.

It is difficult to say what actually occurs when two people create art together. Certainly, it becomes impossible to determine where one vision ends and where the next begins—but there is more to it than that. Images are born, given up for adoption, only to reappear in the garden late at night. Unfamiliar birds squabble in the treetops, and light slants when it hits the water. Orchids die for no reason. Sometimes, a tree will burst into flame the instant a door is opened.

At 3 am on August 24, 2003 the poems written together by Yoko Danno and James C. Hopkins became this book called *The Blue Door.*

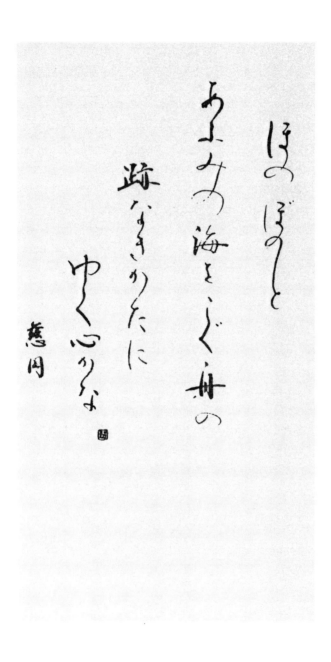

our mind follows
  the boat that rowed out at dawn
    leaving no trace on the luminous lake

Monk Jien (1155-1225)

Contents

The Blue Door ◆ 7

1. children

homecoming ◆ 14
moon dance ◆ 15
tears in the shell ◆ 16
shadow ◆ 17
hopscotch ◆ 18

2. male/female

dreamscape ◆ 20
signs of transformation ◆ 22
seagulls ◆ 24
birthplace ◆ 25
night in the enormous room ◆ 27
visitation ◆ 28
sky womb ◆ 29
moon ◆ 30
drifting off on the boat ◆ 31
rebirth ◆ 32
departure ◆ 33

3. water/fire

release ◆ 36
diving lessons ◆ 38
beachcombing ◆ 40
celestial navigation ◆ 41
anima ◆ 43

ice land ♦ 45
fire offering in benares ♦ 47
spark ♦ 49
ghost ♦ 50

4. between worlds

night heron ♦ 52
message ♦ 54
pearl diving ♦ 55
below the surface ♦ 57
open-air theater in nara ♦ 59
night in benares ♦ 61
click ♦ 62
explosion ♦ 64
when the mist clears ♦ 65
flower offering ♦ 67

5. beyond

the blue door ♦ 70
crystal ♦ 72
mirror ♦ 73
after the tunnel ♦ 74
petals ♦ 76
city spring ♦ 78
evening flower ♦ 79
where did it begin and end? ♦ 80
home is where ♦ 81

Concordance ♦ 83
About the Authors ♦ 84
About International Editions ♦ 86
About the Word Works ♦ 87

I. children

homecoming

i waited
by the white marble window sill
outside the age-old mansion
because i forgot to bring
the key –

i knocked
on the locked door
but nobody answered
though there was light inside –

i kept standing
for eons
until i felt ivy clinging,
climbing
round my rooted body –

thickly mantled
with shiny leaves,
i stretched my limbs
eager for sunshine and water –

overhead a swallow
swept through the deepening blue
and from far below,
gently on a sea breeze,
a boy and a girl whispered,

"we are back home, please let us in,
let us in…"

moon dance

the gale spent –
the torrential rain stopped,
thunderclaps faded,

white clouds torn away
like sheets stripped off the bed,
the full moon is revealed –

a hush falls over the forest,
the translucent curtain rises –
act one, scene one: a hunting preserve –

the girl in a red cap:
"be careful, the keeper of the wood
might find you waving your bow at me."

the boy in a blue scarf:
"how could i stop chasing you?
we've fallen under the moon's spell."

moths flitter in the light
streaming through the trees,
a lullaby floats from
a worn-out music box –

her hands remember
   a thousand stitches
her grandmother made,
   the rhythm of weaving,

shelling oysters and peanuts
   by a fire built in the hearth,
plucking herbs with an awakening smell –
   a hundred burning sensations.

tears in the shell

without calculating
the distance

to the infinite,

flags of five colors
flutter in the breeze,
sending

prayers
like fragrance

from golden flowers
blooming along a mountain pass
that was once the ocean floor –

"those are pearls in your eyes,"
the boy mutters to himself,
still wet from seawater –

"those are tears inside the shells
you are holding for me,"
the girl joins him –

in her eyes
the light
of shooting stars

rushing through dense air.

shadow

the clouds break,
from the deepening dusk
earthen walls appear –

enclosed is a well-kept garden,
lush with gardenias,

tricolor azaleas,
sweet-smelling daphnes
in the shade of fragrant olives,

a bower on the pond
fed by hidden water,
lanterns along the stepping-stones –

a child hops,
skips, and jumps
into the moonlight – *it's easy, mama,*

to go in and out
of your giant shadow.

hopscotch

on a moonlit night
the child alone
is playing hopscotch,

spellbound
by the game, not knowing
it's past time to go home – each time

she kicks the cobblestone
over a line chalked on the street,
she remembers her grandmother saying,

*when you travel to a foreign country
you must cross a border.
when you step into a new land*

*you'll be relieved,
to find an image of yourself,
the one you abandoned in a mirror –*

the child keeps breaking
through the white line,
her shadow hopping behind her

like a twin – *grandma, every
new line leads me to another!*

2. male/female

dreamscape

i was picking up white pebbles,
one by one, on the beach
along a vast river – i barely
held one in my hand when
it began to melt.

a stranger joined me
in collecting pebbles –
soon i knew him
as my primordial mate.

he said,
"i am from
an island yet to be
formed, and badly need
stones rubbed,
smooth and round, rolled
in water."

"what color do you want?" i asked.
"blue," he answered,
"it's the color of the ribbon
my girl once wore
around her wrist

to keep her spirit
from flying
too near a blazing sun."

together with him
i thought deeply of a field
filled with flaming flowers
swaying in a breeze –
and it took form around us.

at the stroke of
twelve, the scene dissolved.
i surfaced – back in circulation.

signs of transformation

i rise with your dreams
still fluttering in my head
and stumble into the bathroom
to shave.
when my bathrobe sash
slips through its loops
i notice that i am covered
in feathers.

i go into the kitchen
to make a cup of tea,
hoping that things
will change.
the water boils quickly.
the tea bag steeps.
the steam feels good
on my face.

when i return
to the bathroom
and look into the mirror
someone has taken my place –
a pale-skinned woman
with eyes like white pearls
who is smiling
and holding my razor.

i touch her left hand.
the glass feels warm.
together,

we trace a circle in the air.
i decide to return
to bed for the day.
sometimes just waking up
can be complicated.

seagulls

today the seagulls returned.
noisy and careening through the marina,
spinning grey cartwheels
above the masts.

it happened so fast,
this change of seasons
caught me sleeping –
lines and wooden blocks
stacked all around,
pulleys overhead.

when our fingers
touch
will our hearts skip
a beat?
will the bed
be stripped
of its sheets?

the seagulls scream
and scatter like leaves,
something has startled
their tiny hearts.
a grey feather falls
through the air
like a whisper,
settling
on wet
white
paint.

birthplace

somehow
    i felt
        over and again
the touch
    of soft summer grass
        crushed under my bare feet –

fireflies gleamed
        around a tall willow tree,
starlight trickled
        along the slender leaves,
            a blue fire
                along my skin,

on
the island,
a thousand wine-colored
waves washing the white shores –

on
the lush mountain
i roamed with a snake
god, my
friend,
        hunting for birds'
            nests –

these scenes i remember
along with
my

twin/mate/partner,

living together
    on the blue-green island,

                            before

    an all-swallowing deluge
                        of lava.

night in the enormous room

when the owl

in the olive trees

whistled

for a lover

the night became

much more than

the thing that you hold.

it became an offering –

a handful of gems. you

with me, miles below,

a cavern of darkness

where everything

was now reflected

in a clear river,

the moon alive

like

for a small sacrifice

the heartbeat of a mouse

pit-pat, pit-pat

quivering in your palm.

so you took it then,

carried it home and

released it into the wild –

into a glittering haven

that was

a garden

fast with fireflies,

 weeping

willow trees,

night birds –

restless

on the tips

of branches.

visitation

the taking
was like the plucking
of an evening flower.
not exactly violent,
but with force
enough.

and now
the thing that courses
through us both
is the same –
our dark and
secret link.

i can think
of nothing
but the blue of your wrist –
the sweet spark
beneath
the skin,

the
palpable richness
singing
through our veins,
just as the flow
begins.

sky womb

                        in a dream last night
                          i swallowed down
                a stone with sweet water – it

passed through the windpipe,
                          slid down the soft passage,
deep into the cave to a pool,
                          into a saltwater oyster,
each time saturated air drips,
                          penetrating the membrane,
the still water slightly moving,
                          with the pulse of rocking time,
coatings of calcite added anew,
                          layers of pearl formed –

                      clean
                  ornament to
              the yin and yang
              gods on the moon
              disc embracing
                in opalescent
                      light.

MOON

new:	not existing before
	in the space
	between eyebrows, the deep
	    round well
	        glistening at the bottom

last quarter:	his bow drawn
	to its full
	extent, way out of orbit
	    the arrow
	        disappears in a flash

full:	beyond her usual
	brilliance
	she passes out of reach
	    of our eyes
	        fading out fixed stars

first quarter:	moving slowly
	eastward
	each day the luminous
	    shadow
	        swelling to a whole

new:	yin and yang
	reversed
	in the golden bowl
	    containing
	        a handful of seed dust

drifting off on the boat

i can't sleep tonight.
there's been a change of weather –
an eastern wind
has cleared out the sky,
a persistent moon
has painted the stateroom,
and my arms
are washed in silver.

if i light the candle
of this tiger hour –
my twin will appear
in the ripple of flame.
she will close my eyes
and draw me to her,
transform us
with familiar light.

underneath the bed
this endless river
runs its fingers
along the ribs of the boat –
lifting us slightly
as it moves through the night,
laying us down
as it passes.

rebirth

even
more rare
than lightning
on a clear day,
to have found
this precious body
again.

no time
for the endless
cities of the mind,
or the tissue
that keeps us
separate.

doves
are whistling
in the darkest eaves.
the moon
has changed
her plans.

daylight
is fleeing
on golden spurs.
come, take this bowl
from my
hand.

departure

yesterday the house was empty –

    wind
            rustled the carpet
                      of dry sedge grass,

    moonlight
            streaming through
                      a cleft of the shingled roof,

    pale grey mist
        hovered on the lake
                hiding incessant ripples –

bamboo leaves
        falling
    in the blink of a star's
                      birth,

white feathers
    scattering,
        the weaver at her loom
                keeps weaving,
                          waiting –

    tonight
        i want
            a clear sky,
    so he
        may wade
            across the milky river.

the earth fleeting
    under their feet,
golden dust of the sun
    swirling in each other's
                arms

at dawn today –

    sleeves
          heavy
                with dew,
    clothes
          exchanged,

    they depart,
          each heading
                for the next

          growing season.

3. water/fire

release

i lost my voice
singing in a chorus last night,

felt a stone
    fall out of the sky,
        through my throat
            and into my heart –

i watched my lips

        floating down the river...

        my hands   my brains...

        my sash...
    my skirt   my shoes...

my letters... my notebooks...

i climbed out of the water
    onto the edge of a steep cliff,
        a stream of torrential light
            flowing over –

eyes
    in the tea leaves
        seeing flags
           transparent
              shimmering on the waves...

ears
    inside the granite
        hearing
            five colors
                fluttering in a breeze...

in a lush garden
    blind fingertips touch
        a moment in ample space...

    singing voices
        of a male and a female
            intertwined rising from

                one throat...

diving lessons

ten years later
i was swimming in stingrays,
    gravity-free on a turquoise neap tide,
parting the water with outstretched arms
      at the final fingers of reef.

the woman i was following
      kicked with alabaster legs
    that led us to the edge
      of the deepest sea
      and then she disappeared from sight.

i can't call it a vacation:
i've been there since birth –
kicking and stroking,
looking for the chance
      to escape through the tiniest opening –
      call it an underwater life.

suddenly the shelf dropped away to navy
      and fifty feet down on a sandy bed
lay a chaos of fallen figures –
      hundreds of broken arms and legs.
        headless bodies,
          splayed in an orgy of marble.

i am not amazed
by the fact that glass
was once the sand on my tongue.
or that one can shatter
      at the bottom of the sea
      just as easy as a dive through a skylight.

but i was surprised
        when she opened her mouth
and revealed the wedding ring i'd given her
        clenched tight in her teeth –
                sparkling as though the thought of loss
                were as distant as the shore itself.

it was then
that the statues got up and swam away,
disappearing into the panes of blue.
the stingrays circled once,
then kited off into the deep.

i floated back up
    and took a job in town,
polishing silver offering bowls
        on sundays, in a seaside church.
            when the sun streams into the sanctuary
            all the windows
                begin to breathe.

ten fathoms down
with a mouthful of air
you can only stay alive for so long.
and glass, like water,
        continues to flow
        long after the heat is gone.

beachcombing

there is nothing new
        under the sun
                and nothing old in the air above it,

    not the white thigh
           of the moon against the sky or
                  the tongue of a thousand waves.

starfish once trapped
        in the tidal pool
                become a skateboard park,

    while the funeral light
           of the long-dark star
                has yet to pierce the night.

we emerge from the sea
        opalescent,
                dripping ancient tales:

salt from the hands
        of a silk road merchant,
                tears from an empress's eyes.

    we walk the shore
           with empty shells
                and listen for the ghost crab's song.

    we trace our names
           at the edge of the sea.
                we turn our backs and they're gone.

celestial navigation

here at the shore
    the water that   raised you
    has laid you back down again.
        and the wake
            that played out
        for miles and miles
has caught up
    and safely
        passed.

the air pulses
      with kelp and canvas.
        the only sound
    is the   *chunk*
          of the bow
bumping
against   sea-smoothed wall.

now the sun
    melts like glass
      out across the piazza.
the painters lift their brushes.
      waiters bend
    and pour once again.
the patrons return
to their salads.

            we are past the point
            of the day's own burning –
      the sun

             has offered up its sister.
    when she arrives,
                 yearning for your gaze,
                      do not treat her like a stranger.

loosen   the lines
   and slip back to the sea.
                let the sheets run free
   until the wind   catches
                and the canvas   lifts and swells.

              then,   with your head thrown back
                                against the sky,

you must flow with
   the pull
       of tide.

tie off the tiller,
   the boat knows where to go.

              night   will return
                         without you.

ANIMA

a wind is blowing
        from the caribbean sea,
                a singer sings sweetly,

on our way home my little girl found a bird,
eyes closed in the wayside shrubbery –
i picked it up and felt it barely breathing,
the feathers soft, ash-green, on my palm –

a woman is
        a rough sea
             quiet down below,
                  she lifts her voice,

the fish jumped off the cutting board,
flopping around on the wooden floor.
with a knife in my hand, frozen, i watched
until the headless carp calmed down –

a woman is
        a turbulent reflection
             of the rumbling sky,
                  the singer softly groans,

the sun glazing the parched fields,
the woman wailed like a wounded animal
that had lost its young, and went out
for food, water and a mate –

a woman is always
        double-hearted,
                the voice is whispering,

we put out to sea – my little girl sets free
the tiniest of the three fish she caught,
and we eat the rest to celebrate her birthday –

a wind is blowing
        on the blue-green sea,
                we breathe in,
            blow into paper balloons,
                    and let them go.

six miles sunward from the north atlantic
a shattered white continent turns beneath us
like the furthest memory of winter.

twin turbines drone against the trade winds,
frozen air screams around our plane,
and tiny crystals inch across the panes.

when asked, you will order red wine.

somewhere below us there must be a man,
dressed in fur, maybe thigh-deep in snow,
moving across the landscape alone.

he leans into the wind, squints in the sunlight,
and is content to occasionally stumble –
he knows this is what is expected.

or maybe white wine this time, for a change.

in order for the man to continue walking
all passengers must return to their seats.
smoking is never permitted.

in order for the plane to continue eastward
the man must sleep beneath stars.
he must eat what he kills.

        for a change, maybe white this time.

below us, the pack-ice shoulders millions of years.
the landscape cracks and reshapes itself,
and the man has forgotten his name.

a shadow plane flickers across the ice.
the man cups his hand to light a cigarette –
surely that match will be his last.

        yes, you will order red wine when asked.

fire offering in benares

from the mountains of ice and warped serac,
    glittering rails snake down to the plains –
    they melt deep into fern and riverside mud,
pool beneath restless palms.

a half-moon lifts above the mercury tracks.
    the sky cracks open like soft black fruit
    spilling stars and the dust of a million moths
        across the sky.

a shadowless train backs into the station
    covered in salt and tattered wings,
    huffing hard as a winded hound.
        a thousand brown hands reach out for tea.
statues of krishna, smiling blue god
        nod in relentless heat.

we quit the train as water would –
    press through haunches, baubles, eons,
    until we arrive at the shore.
    what more could i want, not held in my hands?
        what ashes not yet offered to the wind?

past the river bend, an iron skeleton
    carries the train away –
    it rolls across the rusted bones,
        and vanishes into night.
    a yellow sari whispers to the floor
    in a room above our heads.

the moths of the moon have returned again –
        come to lick at the fire in our hands.
      we lay our flames down on tiny boats
    woven from banana leaves –
a murmur from the lips of the blue-skinned god
          – we send them floating to the sea.

spark

the sun
moves behind
a sky like frosted glass

and spins the day out
like a spool
of grey thread.

from my bed,
i watch
and wait all day,

while the fire in the hearth
casts shapes
on the walls.

the sun
disappears.
the swallows return.

the fire
cracks a spark
onto the floor.

i wait
but she never
returns.

from the faintest
red glow
at the edge of the bed

this blanket
will soon
start to burn.

ghost

i met last night,
between sleep and waking,
a pair of merry ghosts, haunting
a house once buried under volcanic ash.

>   it's an act
>   of super-human love
>   that transforms
>   nightmare into bliss –

>   shattered glass
>   fell like flaming arrows
>   from the grey sky
>   turning into
>   white flower petals –

>   somehow in excavation,
>   the moment air touches
>   the sealed interior,
>   fragrance rises
>   from the cavities
>   left by evaporated bodies.

i sensed spirits, dancing wild
in the closed chamber,
almost within reach

heard a boy and a girl laughing
in response to birds calling
in a long-destroyed garden.

4. between worlds

night heron

tonight,
in the marina,
the river
is like a mirror.
the powerboats
lie still
on black water.
not a breath.
not a ripple.
no sound.

sometimes
this shadowy,
floating world
is held together
by dream.
in the moment
where rising
meets falling
the seam
becomes
almost intangible.

a night heron
perched
on a wooden piling
cocks her head
as i pass.
i wave my hand
in the air
like a wand,
but she doesn't
desert her post.

a movement,
a shadow,
has caught her eye –
something
drifting
into the light.

she folds her wings
to pierce
the dark surface,
and drops
out of sight.

message

a legend tells
where a sage thrust
his stick, a hot spring appeared –

monkeys, deer, bears and birds,
occasionally a few humans,
come to the spa surrounded by rocks,
to cure their wounds –

i cast a net for thrush
in a flurry of falling cherry blossoms,
a woven lace of light –

i fix my eyes on my flickering reflection
watching me from the depths
of the clear hot water,

asking me: *who are you?*
where are you from? why here?
a baboon, burglar, solitary wanderer,

fiddler, lunatic, secret
messenger from the land
of the dead?

nightly, translucent feathers fall
on my bed. i strain my eyes
to see the words written on them.

pearl diving

i clapped my hands   twice   for protection,
twirled the sky around my head,
   then, seeing my reflection,
   dove
   right in –
surprised   when i disappeared.

water and air are the same in their blueness
yet can only reflect each other   for so long.
      sooner or later   the horizon   is broken –
            the elements become
one.

when your eyes become mine
i will sweep the hearth with a heather broom,
         check the pulse in the upstairs bedroom,
                  take the children to the park.

                  when my hands become yours
         you'll send the shirts out to be pressed.
you'll submit a request for the latest data,
telephone empty streets.

the mist   waited in vain   all night
swooned   into sea
                  this   morning.
and the clouds that moved across its surface
now dream only of
                  rain.

   if i drop
the knife   that i grasp in my hand
                            it will disappear without
                            a sound.

it will pierce   through
      this world
      as it enters the next –

pulling sunlight
                          all the way down.

below the surface

*you have to be very careful
    when you uncover the lid:
    the moment anything touches
    open air, the colors
        change and begin
                to crumble –*

    *a flower wreath offered,
    rosemary and thyme
    woven together,*

    *a wooden coffin
    buried fathoms deep
    in the wet stratum,
    foliage intact.*

*in searching for things lost
        in the depth of sea
    you must keep your eyes
    open, dive slowly
    and calmly,
    but don't forget to breathe
    only through your mouth*

    *otherwise
pressure increases,
and bubbles expand
critically
in your blood –*

a missing
knife
retrieved
from a shark's jaw

a moon hidden
in a midsummer dream
found in an octopus'
trap.

open-air theater in Nara

i was on my way to the shrine in the depth of a wood for the music and dancing offered to the gods of light. the long graveled path was filled with thousands carrying lanterns. when i was about to be swept off by the crowd you reached out to me and took my hand. we waded together through the jostling worshippers to the open-air theater and took our seats. it had stopped raining and a half moon shone between the clouds. the birds had long ceased to sing. it was quiet like the bottom of the sea.

    the vapor condenses
                droplets
  release
                    evaporate anew

        the grey curtain is torn
    open

with an untimely shower
   of cicadas'
      chirps
       between the fingers
 of a tree
stars feebly shine

        a woman
      slips out
    through
   the painted
  paper door
        wearing green leaves

                                                    in her hair

        she crosses the threshold   of a fleeting portal
                                dancing
                    to silver bells
                        and deerskin drums
                            on islands of clouds

            the twin shadows   of stone lanterns
waiting for
                        the sky   to clear
                insects
                    in shells
                        like night

                                    the five senses, dormant
                            through eight light years
    emerge from the earth,

                            feelers   swaying in a breeze

                                from her waving fan

night in benares

by the time we reached benares we had almost run out of money, so we slept on the whitewashed roof of the hotel. for a few rupees we spread out our blankets and waited for the night to join us. lulled by a dreadlocked israeli with a battered guitar lounging in a cloud of blue smoke, we listened as the ancient city staggered off to bed. laughter, and the fading shouts of night vendors. cats hunting shadows, and the hum of air conditioners. our fingers just touching as we drifted off together:

it snows for days
and drifts high
until the stone animals
in the garden are
completely buried.

in the pale sunlight
the children carve out caves
and curl up
in their secret lairs.

muffled in whiteness
and out of sight
they can almost hear
the flakes
piling up outside.

all afternoon
beneath the snow,
the sound
of tiny breathing.

groaning,
clanking
from side to side,
a train like an elephant
pounds through rajasthan.

water buffaloes
black and crusted in mud,
plod
beside the shimmering rails.

at the riverbank
they slap at flies
with their tails
and sink
beneath the surface.

a bright yellow sari.
an ankle bracelet
that sparkles
in the sun.

click

i was busy washing dishes
and clothes in the river,
the sun glaring down on me,

there wasn't a breath
of wind, the bright yellow sari
clinging to my thighs,

the ancient grey path
leading into the unfamiliar wood,
covered with mica dust –

i heard a click
like a door opened
deep inside a house,

but only saw
a mouse scurrying away
from the muddy ditch –

the next time it
happened
i was climbing,

gasping for breath,
heading for the cloud-hidden
winter peak,

the instant i sensed a click on my back
i was sliding down the precipice
at frightful speed,

the safety rope
broken, my ice axe
useless –

on the soft
snow piles i woke to a delirium:
a naked sinewy man

burning in the floating desert,
cold flames flaring up,
the tongue of a thousand waves –

this morning i caught accidentally
the crisp moment a lotus
bud

    popped
            open
                      in the pale sunlight.

explosion

a promise of fine weather,
flashes of lightning in the purple sky
above the luminous crystal city,

a persistent rumbling
in my dull head before waking
or in a rain cloud below the horizon –

i heard someone treading
softly on grapes – droplets seeping
into layers of my dream…fermenting…

and before dawn something
rich exploded in my sleep
or in a fireworks factory –

for generations behind my back
mountains being mined
for gold…drilled…blasted…into debris…

a tricky moment
of cave-in
passed,

flaming butterflies
frightened
settled,

the balance
regained

deep
inside
the bedrock.

when the mist clears

a map of the world above my bed,
i woke in china, with a mind of bamboo,
and my legs curled around you –
like night gone to bloom,
like sunday, or the need for rice.

my head is like a tiny quail
still fluttering in a snare of silk.
there're a lot of things i'd do for tea –
getting up isn't one of them.

two floors down,
today's radio is deciding what to wear.
it licks at the air and chooses a highway
without another truck for miles.

someone dumps a basket of glass
down the garbage chute.
the churchgoing pigeons are wrong once again.
the elevator is finally stuck.

you shift in your sleep
like distant dark music.
when the light hits your face
you will remember kowloon
and the river like a shaving mirror.

mangoes. plum wine. root vegetables in the crisper –
there are worse things to be
than prepared.

later this morning, when the mist lifts,
two things
will suddenly become clear:

the way the land curves out
like the small of your back
all along the lee.
and the way a boat
rowed out from the harbor
leaves no trace
on the sea.

flower offering

                          a tiny
                    white rose bud
          is an impossible peak
           to the mite that lives
                      in its folds.

to this pale
and stubborn life
i now return
all the colors
i've stolen.

s. beyond

the blue door

having passed through
the blue door
of the pool's deepest end
we hover
in its turquoise room.
in these liquid moments,
suspended in the glistening,
we abandon
our sciences
and selves.

we sink or rise
with the prize of breath,
give way
to the gentle horizontal.
we encounter
our new bodies
in stroke and ripple,
and converse
in murmur
and eep.

the kindness of water
is its closeness
to death,
and the drowning
that we don't have to do.
the truth of water
is in its sending us sunward,
back up
through the glittering blue door.

we hold tight
to the edge
with our fingertips –
a momentary
warming of the skin.
but the towel stays folded,
the lawn chair
empty.
we breathe,
and let go again.

crystal

past the point of no return,
our jet trails
sparkling white claw marks –

   last night a burglar tore
     a page from my unraveled
             mystery book,

"how can you find
   a flower blooming
      in an icy lake?"
           the missing page says –

the moment
   a hand touches a hand,
     palm to palm,
       skin to skin
            under clear fresh water,

vapor rises
   from soft wet leaves,
     condenses into
           a blue orchid…freezes…

as we fly higher
through air strata
to the home of the stars
the temperature falls.

not even a blanket,
nor the heat of blood circulating
through a polar bear scratching the air
can melt the flower in ice.

mirror

on visiting her old home,	in quest of ancestral roots
her eyes,	his eyes,
looking through	looking for her
the lattice door,	through the
see	still
familiar landscapes	surface of crystal
inside	water,
unchanged;	unstirred
the same old pine tree towering	in the limestone cave, radiate
aslant	a glow;
over the garden,	leaves unshaken
man-made	by the wind,
dry river, a stone bridge	a dark-red tree, unconcerned
five feet across,	by the noise of
the stepping stones	cicadas, stands behind
in overgrown moss;	tombs underwater;
the aged rocks	absorbing light
her great-grandmother	from above, the pool turns
transported in three	into a cold jewel, their
carloads, mostly to be buried,	hands gleam as she dives after
some to furnish the garden,	him searching for pearl shells;
look shrunken,	bubbles rise
the surrounding trees	as the inhaled air
and azalea bushes	burns the thirsty
grown taller,	blood in their
twelve zodiac animals	bodies; needing breath,
carved	missing
around the stone	animals sneak out
lantern,	from their
lost	lairs

after the tunnel

waves of heat
    above the railroad track
        shimmer ahead,

the sea glittering
    with light reflected
        from the turning sky,

our train running
    along the coast of a thousand-ri
        into the afterglow,

forward and backward,
    our bodies respond
        to the sleep-inducing vibration –

at the dingy
    countryside station
             we were to get off

    in time for supper tonight –

one chance lost, but
    small affairs return
        in eccentric orbits
            like star dust

    in a galactic system:

             drippings
        from   fingertips
    alabaster throats   peach   pink blossoms

        breakfast   on the beach
     flamingos   pomegranates   gems –

we fell asleep
     dreaming together
          a meteoric dream
              of a bright celestial body
                    with a tail
   piercing the void,
       just for three seconds,

    and missed again
         our station...too late...

          and there's no way
   to retrieve
      the old
        familiar
          senses.

petals

stems

                    swimming
   throat

intertwine just
                          moon

   silver as fish and

   blue in the

reflected

        sky, to return as rain

offering ourselves to the dream

padme hum...om mani padme

even glass is made peaceful again

    fingertips

of monks, forehead to flagstone

weave water with

forever.   taste this
                           and remember the sea

        into bliss.

lie back in the arms of
open the sky
again and again. ten thousand

            jewels, wound around the sun

trace the fissures
                    of the furthest mountain

eyes closed – saving the sky
from too much of itself.

and stars   that cannot be spent.

city spring

there isn't a tree outside my apartment,
but there should be.

  it should wake with first light
    in these new mornings, and –
          raising its pink fists into the air –
      shout emerald manifestos
          at early passers-by,
  while the pigeon-lady
            shakes out her seeds

i need roots now.
something sturdy enough to climb –

  rough and nascent
      with a pastel sense of time, and
          a name i can't pronounce.
something determined
            to rise
                above the aerials.

there isn't a tree outside my apartment,
but i'm hoping.

  last night   i threw all the windows open,
      and set a bowl of water on the sill.
          say what you will about superstition –
            the day blossomed in azure.
now the pigeon-lady sings
      as she empties her bag.

    the sky
      is filled

with wings.

evening flower

a wind suddenly clears off the clouds –
the moon is ominously bright
after the earth's shadow has passed –

we go up the winding stone steps
to the old castle garden, slightly drunk
from red wine, and touch

a tall tree spreading out
its branches,
for help –

year in
the ancient tree sheds leaves,
year out
it sprouts –

am i a leaf that falls,
or a part
of the trunk that yields
a seed?

are you a dream
fallen from the enormous
bulk of shadows,

or are you
from the bright source
of darkness?

we look into each other's eyes
and hesitate a moment before entering
the blue shining
center

of expanding light.

where did it begin and end?

                              i

            looked left   looked right

           before my eyes   adjusted

            the horizon   to the light

            stretched out   and opened

            further than   imagination into

           the edges of   something wide

            the song   did it seem that

       i had sung to myself   for a lifetime

           a reminder   of silence

             of just   how near or

             how far   finally

           we had come   far didn't matter

            together   we had only to stay

          or had to go   you were

            you and   ultimately

                              i

home is where

my first few footprints
    have now filled with rain
        and flowers blown in
            from the garden next door.

        my guidebook
           recommended
              breakfast bars, locks,
                  and tiny tablets –

              in the end
                i brought
                only
                  air.

                  just
                  space
                  for
                  vision,

            and my special
            reverse-camera
          that only takes photos
       of my eyes.

      no martini anecdotes
    of peril and wonder,
no answers to all the
cocktail questions –

did you have a...?
    did you visit...?

well, when i was...
well, there used to...

      no tinctures or unguents
         for new breeds of bugs,
            no handmade journals
              in optimistic color.

                i am carrying
              a peach and a
                transparent
                passport

                and
                the woman
                in the photo
              is my twin.

           i have paced off the landscape
        one bead at a time.
      i have determined
      the curve of the sky.

      i approach the house backwards.
    the door is an ocean.
  i reach for the handle and
step into light.

concordance

by Yoko Danno:

by James C. Hopkins:

homecoming	signs of transformation
moon dance	seagulls
tears in the shell	night in the enormous room
shadow	visitation
hopscotch	drifting off on the boat
dreamscape	rebirth
birthplace	diving lessons
sky womb	beachcombing
moon	celestial navigation
departure	ice land
release	fire offering in benares
anima	spark
ghost	night heron
message	pearl diving
below the surface	night in benares
open-air theater in nara	when the mist clears
click	flower offering
explosion	the blue door
crystal	petals
mirror	city spring
after the tunnel	where did it begin and end?
evening flower	home is where

about James C. Hopkins

JAMES C. HOPKINS was born in Washington, DC and raised in the Blue Ridge mountains of Virginia. He studied French language and literature at Duke University, and he has twice received scholarships for poetry study at The George Washington University. He has written two previous books of poetry—a chapbook entitled *The Walnut Tree Waits for Its Bees* (1997), and a full-length book entitled *Eight Pale Women* (2003). His poems have appeared in numerous journals and anthologies, including *Heliotrope, Baltimore Review* and *Potomac Review*.

These days, James splits his time between Washington, DC, where he works as an investment broker, and Kathmandu, Nepal, where he studies Buddhist philosophy and Himalayan languages at a Tibetan monastery.

About Yoko Danno

YOKO DANNO was born, raised, and educated in Japan. A graduate of Kobe College, she has been writing poetry solely in English. In addition to being a poet, she is also a playwright, translator, and editor of The Ikuta Press in Kobe, Japan. Her long poem, "Four Songs" was published in the *International Anthology of Poetry and Prose 47* by New Directions, New York. She is the author of four books of poetry: *trilogy, Hagoromo: A Celestial Robe, Dusty Mirror* all published by The Ikuta Press, Kobe, and *Epitaph for Memories* published by The Bunny and the Crocodile Press, Washington, DC. Her translation of *The Kojiki, Record of Ancient Matters*, Japan's oldest extant mythology and chronicle compiled in the 8th century, will be published by Ahadada Books, Toronto/Tokyo, in the summer of 2006. She lives in Kobe with her family.

AUTHORS' PHOTO BY MARNI KRAVITZ

about International Editions

INTERNATIONAL EDITIONS is an imprint of The Word Works. *The Blue Door* is the fourth book in this series. The following people have helped make this book possible:

PATRONS
Akitsu Nagasawa • Asako Iida • Robert E. Brailsford • Gene L. Colombini • Robert & Lucy Cook • Kazuko Hatano • Myong-Hee Kim • Joanna & Steve King • Rick & Becky Klein • Judith McCombs • Miles David Moore • Seiichi Iida • Aaron & Laura Strubel • Jonathan Vaile • Charlotte Warren

DONORS
Karren L. Alenier • Elaine Arena & Jim Dykes • Scott & Sonja Beebe • Carl Bolyard & Larisa Wells • John & Beverly Hines • Elinor & Jim Hopkins • Eiko Isano • Masako Furuya • Michiko Konishi • Hiroko Nakagawa • Satoko Nishioka • Yoshiko Noguchi • Jill Tunick • Anne-Marie Urban

FRIENDS
John Ackerly • Nancy & Dan Allen • Robert Allred • Mel Belin • Martha B. Bishop • Ron Blasing • Jennifer Daniels & Karen Murph • Tim Gammon • Paul Grayson • Marilyn Kravitz • Chris Llewellyn • Tay Louden • Suzanne Lucas

Special thanks to the many anonymous contributors.

about the Word Works

The WORD WORKS, a nonprofit literary organization, publishes contemporary poetry in collectors' editions. Since 1981, the organization has sponsored the Washington Prize, a $1,500 award to an American poet. Monthly, The Word Works presents free literary programs in the Chevy Chase Café Muse series, and each summer, free poetry programs are held at the historic Joaquin Miller Cabin in Washington, DC's Rock Creek Park. Annually, two high school students debut in the Miller Cabin Series as winners of the Jacklyn Potter Young Poets Competition.

Since 1974, WORD WORKS programs have included: "In the Shadow of the Capitol," a symposium and archival project on the African-American intellectual community in segregated Washington, DC; the Gunston Arts Center Poetry Series (Ai, Carolyn Forché, Stanley Kunitz, and others); the Poet-Editor panel discussions at the Bethesda Writer's Center (John Hollander, Maurice English, Anthony Hecht, Josephine Jacobsen, and others); Poet's Jam, a multi-arts program series featuring poetry in performance; a poetry workshop at the Center for Creative Non-Violence (CCNV) shelter; and the Arts Retreat in Tuscany. Master Class workshops, an ongoing program, have featured Agha Shahid Ali, Thomas Lux, and Marilyn Nelson.

In 2006, The WORD WORKS will have published 60 titles, including work from such authors as Deirdra Baldwin, J.H. Beall, Christopher Bursk, John Pauker, Edward Weismiller, and Mac Wellman. Currently, The Word Works publishes books and occasional anthologies under three imprints: the Washington Prize, the Hilary Tham Capital Collection, and International Editions.

Past grants have been awarded by the National Endowment for the Arts, National Endowment for the Humanities, DC Commission on the Arts & Humanities, Witter Bynner Foundation, Writer's Center, Bell Atlantic, Batir Foundation, and others, including many generous private patrons.

The WORD WORKS has established an archive of artistic and administrative materials in the Washington Writing Archive housed in the George Washington University Gelman Library.

Please enclose a self-addressed, stamped envelope with all inquiries.

The Word Works   PO Box 42164   Washington, DC 20015
   editor@wordworksdc.com   www.wordworksdc.com

Word Works Books

   Karren L. Alenier, *Wandering on the Outside*
   Karren L. Alenier, Hilary Tham, Miles David Moore, eds.,
      Winners: A Retrospective of the Washington Prize
* Nathalie F. Anderson, *Following Fred Astaire*
* Michael Atkinson, *One Hundred Children Waiting for a Train*
   Mel Belin, *Flesh That Was Chrysalis* (CAPITAL COLLECTION)
* Carrie Bennett, *biography of water*
* Peter Blair, *Last Heat*
   Doris Brody, *Judging the Distance* (CAPITAL COLLECTION)
   Grace Cavalieri, *Pinecrest Rest Haven* (CAPITAL COLLECTION)
   Christopher Conlon, *Gilbert and Garbo in Love*
   (CAPITAL COLLECTION)
   Donna Denizé, *Broken Like Job* (CAPITAL COLLECTION)
   Moshe Dor, Barbara Goldberg, Giora Leshem, eds.,
      The Stones Remember
* Linda Lee Harper, *Toward Desire*
   James C. Hopkins, *Eight Pale Women* (CAPITAL COLLECTION)
* Ann Rae Jonas, *A Diamond Is Hard But Not Tough*
   Myong-Hee Kim, *Crow's Eye View: The Infamy of Lee Sang,*
      Korean Poet (INTERNATIONAL EDITIONS)
   Vladimir Levchev, *Black Book of the Endangered Species*
      (INTERNATIONAL EDITIONS)
* Richard Lyons, *Fleur Carnivore*
* Fred Marchant, *Tipping Point*
   Judith McCombs, *The Habit of Fire* (CAPITAL COLLECTION)
* Ron Mohring, *Survivable World*
   Miles David Moore, *The Bears of Paris* (CAPITAL COLLECTION)
   Miles David Moore, *Rollercoaster* (CAPITAL COLLECTION)
   Jacklyn Potter, Dwaine Rieves, Gary Stein, eds.
      Cabin Fever: Poets at Joaquin Miller's Cabin
* Jay Rogoff, *The Cutoff*
   Robert Sargent, *Aspects of a Southern Story*
   Robert Sargent, *A Woman From Memphis*
* Enid Shomer, *Stalking the Florida Panther*
   Maria Terrone, *The Bodies We Were Loaned* (CAPITAL COLLECTION)
   Hilary Tham, *Bad Names for Women* (CAPITAL COLLECTION)
   Hilary Tham, *Counting* (CAPITAL COLLECTION)
   Jonathan Vaile, *Blue Cowboy* (CAPITAL COLLECTION)
* Miles Waggener, *Phoenix Suites*

      * Washington Prize winners